Moments in Eden

For Joyce - On Easter Day, April 7, 1996.
with love from your mom.

Moments in Eden

GARDEN

PHOTOGRAPHS

BY

Richard Brown

Houghton Mifflin Company

BOSTON · NEW YORK

In memory of my son Jonathan,
who taught me the real meaning
of the word love

———

For information about permission to reproduce selections from this book,
write to Permissions, Houghton Mifflin Company, 215 Park Avenue South,
New York, New York 10003.

For information about this and other Houghton Mifflin trade and reference
books and multimedia products, visit The Bookstore at Houghton Mifflin
on the World Wide Web at http://www.hmco.com/trade/.

ISBN 0-395-77186-2
CIP data is available.

PRINTED IN ITALY

SFE 10 9 8 7 6 5 4 3 2 1

Contents

Introduction

Moments in Eden is a collection of garden photographs reflecting man's earthly and universal search for a paradise regained. Some of the gardens portrayed here are the most well known examples of their kind: Versailles, Keukenhof, Sissinghurst, and Tenjuan. Others are as nameless as a Swiss window box and as simple as a single wysteria vine clinging to the timeworn stones of a Cotswold cottage wall.

Because each culture's idea of paradise is unique, man's longing to recreate his own Eden through the ideal garden has expressed itself in endless and often contradictory forms — from the grottoes and cypress avenues of Renaissance Italy, to the elegantly geometric parterres of baroque France, to the sweeping romantic landscapes of eighteenth-century England, filled with sparkling lakes, shaded oak groves, and wandering herds of diminutive deer. The Japanese even perfected a style of garden meant to be visited primarily at night — moonviewing gardens where conical mounds of raked sand glow eerily against darkened pine boughs.

The photographs in this book are meant to examine and celebrate quiet moments of discovery. Photography has its own extraordinary way of altering reality. Out of the fleeting passage of time, the camera can select one moment and grace it with permanence. It can transform a fountain's constant splash of water into translucent sheets of frozen liquid, or preserve the fading perfection of a tulip's bloom.

Over the past decade I have spent countless hours in gardens throughout the world searching with my camera for times when a garden might reveal itself, moments that show its genius, its cultural spirit, its whimsical or sedate nature. Gardens are magical places, and eventually, often mysteriously, a garden will disclose its human creator's vision of an attainable earthly paradise. In the brief instant the shutter is open, I will try to capture these moments in Eden.

Bagatelle

La Roseraie de Bagatelle, the *belle époque* rose garden on the outskirts of Paris, is as thoroughly French and as exuberantly rococo as a painting by Fragonard. Immodestly decorative, ornamented with roses of every conceivable shape and color, it is a place where pure, sensate enjoyment is commended and frivolity is not a crime.

A gazebo sits on a slight rise at one end of the garden — a Victorian confection like the top of a wedding cake, painted the pale blue-green color of a luna moth's wing. Not long ago I spent the better part of a June afternoon there, enjoying the extravagant profusion of roses and, perhaps more, the people who had come to see the giddy spectacle.

Elegantly dressed Parisian couples walked arm in arm, au pair girls pushing baby carriages stopped to gossip, and children scooped up handfuls of fallen petals and threw them like gaudy snowflakes at one another. Only the gardeners in their faded blue work clothes, who clipped and weeded and pruned industriously, bore an earnest mien. The faint fragrance of roses hung in the air like an invisible cloud.

I heard the crunch of approaching footsteps on the gravel walk, and the tapping of a cane. A blind man, accompanied by a young girl — I sensed she was his granddaughter — made his way along the path below the gazebo. He moved without hesitation until, quite abruptly, he stopped at one rose bush with blooms the shade of a conch shell's lining. Wary of the thorns, he grasped a stem just below the flower with two fingers, and slowly bending forward in a ritual I had witnessed many times that afternoon, he gently inhaled its scent.

Clearly he knew this particular rose, recognized its fragrance apart from that of all others. It was a former acquaintance, though for what reason I could only guess. A memory that bloomed each summer in an unseen world, honored with an old man's bow.

The English Gardener

The English gardener has created gardens that are envied the world over. Yes, he has been favored by an unusually benign climate and a richly varied terrain. But it is his character, more than simple good fortune, that has produced such a breathtaking legacy.

Consider for a moment this gardener's clothing: a tweed cap, laundered white shirt, slightly frayed but perfectly presentable cardigan sweater, twill trousers — proper attire, really, more proper than you or I would choose for working in the dirt, but in his case entirely appropriate. For these are clothes that bespeak both comfort and respect for the task at hand. The best English gardens, like the best English country houses, where the dogs are allowed to sleep on the living-room chairs, have this same sense of relaxed formality.

Bred into the English gardener, too, is a sheer delight, an innate eye and boundless enthusiasm for all things horticultural. He possesses the ability to look at a plant in a completely fresh way and place it in brilliant apposition to others, creating combinations of textures, colors, and shapes that form virtuoso passages in the garden. I have seen common wildflowers that I took for granted at home, marsh marigolds or Indian poke, mixed into an English garden in a more formal way, and been as startled by their beauty as I would by a rare orchid.

Finally, in an English gardener, the quiet confidence of a craftsman is evident — the unhurried concentration of someone completely at ease in his work. English gardens aren't tended as much as they are crafted, with deftly trimmed hedges and cordonned fruit trees, lush perennial borders, weed-free and inconspicuously staked when necessary, crisply raked gravel walks, and precisely edged lawns — all done with a sense of exactness that is as keen-edged as this gardener's well-honed sickle blade.

Wilder Edens

The American gardens I find most moving are the gardens that, like America itself, are contradictory and still tinged with wildness. They hint at what was once the natural plenitude, hope, and wonder of a new, untamed world.

I have felt this wildness in seeing dogwood blossoms light up the dark pine woods of Callaway Gardens with a galaxy of starlike flowers, or when the myriad bare branches of beech trees gleamed like silver filigree work on the valley walls of Winterthur. I have felt it watching flocks of wild geese land on the lake at Old Westbury Gardens, breaking the reflections on the mirrored surface of the water into rippling shards of color.

I remember, especially, the wildness when walking through the last remnants of California's great wildflower fields, which are preserved at Antelope Valley. Sheets of solid bloom — gilias and lupines, coreopsis, oenothera, poppies, and desert dandelions — stretched unbroken from my feet to the horizon. In the distance the softly contoured hills appeared to be covered with strangely colored velvet, purple intermingled with yellow, and here and there bright splashes of pure orange.

At first I was afraid to walk through this growth, afraid to crush so many flowers with each footfall. I took only a few cautious steps. Then I grew bolder and waded out into the midst of the knee-deep mass, as it rippled in the wind, stirring up clouds of bees and an occasional songbird. I luxuriated in the wildness of the place as hawks circled overhead and a snake slid quickly from sight between the crowded flower stalks. This to me was America's Versailles, her Wakehurst — a wilder Eden more appropriate to the American spirit than the most perfectly contrived garden could ever be, and one that would never need weeding.

Tenjuan

The art of gardening in Japan has always been one of understatement. The essential elements of rock, water, sand, moss, and meticulously pruned trees are used to convey a feeling of enduring natural harmony. The basic concept of these gardens has remained unchanged for over five centuries. Simple almost to the point of plainness, yet incredibly beautiful, their purpose is to separate the visitor from the distractions of the everyday world and bring heightened awareness to the immediate moment.

Let me describe several minutes in the garden of the Tenjuan temple at the eastern edge of Kyoto. Although behind the walls the rumble of traffic is evident, the sense of apartness from the city is strongly felt. Rising above the camellias and bamboo thickets that screen the edge of the garden, the borrowed scenery of Mount Higashiyama's wooded hillsides emphasizes the feeling of isolation.

This garden meant for stillness and contemplation is, paradoxically, filled with life and motion. In the pond four fat carp swim by in succession, the deeply scalloped pattern of their scales reminiscent of a screen painting. Tiny water birds dart in and out of the stream that feeds the pond, and brown doves with blue-ringed necks strut along the stone path. A girl in a kimono is having her photograph taken. At the path's end a black-robed monk enters, bows and smiles in passing, and stops to study an inscription. A bell sounds; the garden is about to close.

First one, then three snowy egrets appear overhead, having left their feeding at the Kamogawa River, where groups of old men fish with long poles. They cleave the evening air with heavy strokes of their wings, circle once, glowing crimson-edged in the setting sun's final blaze, settle to roost in the tallest pine, and shake off the fading pink light as if it were dust.

Giverny: The Stolen Apple

At Giverny more than any other garden I have visited, the presence of the designer's hand is felt. Giverny, once the home of Monet, is a unique garden that could only stem from a unique intellect. After he purchased Giverny, Monet's gardening and his painting became so inextricably mixed that they seemed to be a single creative process. One difference remained however: when he painted he was often anguished, plagued by moodiness and self-doubt; when he gardened he was filled with joy.

One fall evening, after the throng of tourists had returned to Paris, I found myself alone in the part of the garden that lies directly in front of Monet's pink and blue-green house. There was a feeling, startlingly palpable, that the artist was still present, that he might return any minute, perhaps from capturing the lilac-hued light on the water-lily pond a few steps across the roadway.

Just to my right, several small apples hung from an old tree. It occurred to me that Monet must have planted this tree. It was more likely that Felix Breuil, his head gardener, did the actual work, but for the sake of poetic license I chose to picture the stout figure of Monet himself, the ever-present crumpled cigarette emerging from somewhere within that Santa Claus beard, as he bent over the sapling and smoothed the dirt with his hands.

I had seen this tree only in the spring, laden with blossoms, and had assumed it was mostly decorative — yielding, if any at all, fruit both hard and piercingly bitter. Glancing around to be sure I was alone, I reached over and picked the best-looking apple. Hesitantly, I took a bite. The skin snapped; the flesh was firm. It was delicious.

Geraniums and Cowbells

I once lived in a small Swiss farming village long enough to realize that two unwritten laws are in effect in rural Switzerland. The first decrees that every cow must wear a bell — a very large bell. I soon grew used to, in fact enjoyed, the deep, clanging plainsong, as the cattle were led out to pasture and back, tolling the passing of each summer's day.

The other unwritten law declares that every window ledge must be decorated with geraniums — abundant geraniums. A few sills were empty, it is true, looking as gaping as a missing tooth in an otherwise perfect smile. But in almost every building, a barely contained cascade of geraniums spilled forth from each window. In the evening when I took walks up the narrow road past the old stucco houses and hip-roofed wooden barns to the beech woods, I saw the farmers and their wives watering and pruning, pinching and prodding their plants into full bloom.

I witnessed the unfortunate consequences of following only the spirit and not the letter of these two laws on a July morning when I stopped at a neighbor's farm for a dozen fresh eggs. This farm in particular was always resplendent with geraniums, but it was a little lax about cowbells. I arrived in the cobbled courtyard at just the moment that Madame LaJoinie and her son had rounded up two errant Brown Swiss cows who had escaped from their pasture the night before, and not wearing bells, had been able with total stealth and under cover of darkness to do the things that cows do when they get loose.

Every geranium within cow's reach, those on the first floor windowsills of both house and barn, and those that had once bloomed in pots now broken and tipped over, had been devoured. A high-water mark of bovine destruction could be traced around the farmyard from sill to sill. In a fittingly Swiss version of justice and order, the absence of cowbells had produced an absence of geraniums. The cows now stood before us unrepentant and nonchalant, oblivious to the red flower petals that still clung to their wet noses. *C'est la vie!*

Versailles

Most garden statues I have seen are simply decorative. Those at Versailles, however, are such obvious works of art, with a presence and life of their own, that they seem capable of movement, especially if the circumstances are right. This was the case on one memorable October night as the full moon inched its way above the ornate silhouette of the chateau. The gardeners had left long ago, after sweeping up fallen leaves with their twig brooms and setting the piles on fire. The air was thick with the bittersweet smell, and the still-smoldering ashes glowed faintly in the darkness. Bats appeared, skimming over the reflecting pools, as the figures of the ghostlike marble statues slowly emerged from the darkness in the thin, cold light.

Everywhere they stood: in silent rows, on pedestals, adorning fountains, singly, and in elaborate groups — the Sun King's gods and goddesses — waiting like motionless players on a darkened stage for the play to begin. As broken clouds passed quickly over the moon's face, the statues flickered, appeared, and disappeared, and in the wavering light actually moved, or at least that was the effect of the visual trickery. The muffled voices of other visitors hidden by darkness and the whispered cadence of their footsteps as they climbed the vast staircase leading out of the garden only added to the eeriness of this illusory animation.

As I made my way toward the exit — for the gates were about to close — I paused to look at the statue of Latona and her children that has always been my favorite. There is something especially appealing and lifelike about the gentle tilt of her head and the graceful curve of her extended arm. She stood just above me; far too close to give any false appearance of movement. But as I passed by, she held in her outstretched hand, for just one moment, the perfect silver sphere of the rising moon.

Holland's Flower

In the early seventeenth century, men with starched, ruffled collars in Amsterdam and Haarlem and Delft were possessed by the allure of the tulip's silken bloom. Tulips had caused great excitement in Holland when they were first brought from Turkey some fifty years earlier, but the tulip mania that swept the country in the 1630s had more to do with greed than horticulture.

Bulb growers discovered that on rare occasions ordinary tulips could develop flowers of exceptional and unpredictable beauty, flowers with lustrously striped and marbled petals or wildly colored, feathered blooms. We know now that these spectacular mutations were caused by a plant virus, but to the Dutch burghers it seemed like a miracle — a miracle worth betting on. As rare tulips became the rage among Holland's wealthy, speculation in tulip bulbs became a national obsession.

I picture these Dutch bulb speculators in Vermeer rooms softly illuminated by northern light flowing in from a high window onto the tiled floor, sitting by a rug-draped table, coveting that one, ultimately glorious tulip with petals more precious than beaten gold. I think of them daydreaming as they hold the dormant, onionlike bulb in their hands, wondering what future marvel might unfold from within its dry papery skin. Such men, in a moment of weakness, could spend two or three thousand florins for a single handful of bulbs. For a few uncertain years an economy revolved around a flower — a mad, wonderful, short-lived accident of nature and history too much like an operetta to last. As the passion for rare tulips waned among the rich, the market became flooded with overpriced bulbs and soon collapsed. The government, seeing so many of its citizens facing ruin, outlawed future tulip speculation.

Today the mischievous, wonder-working virus can be introduced and controlled scientifically, and tulips colored like birds of paradise can be produced as easily as any other. Still, to see Holland's bulb fields bloom in the spring, blanketing the lowlands with a patchwork of color — field after field of tulips, alizarin crimson and brilliant orange, dusky purple and clarion yellow — is to understand how, once, men valued them more than gold.

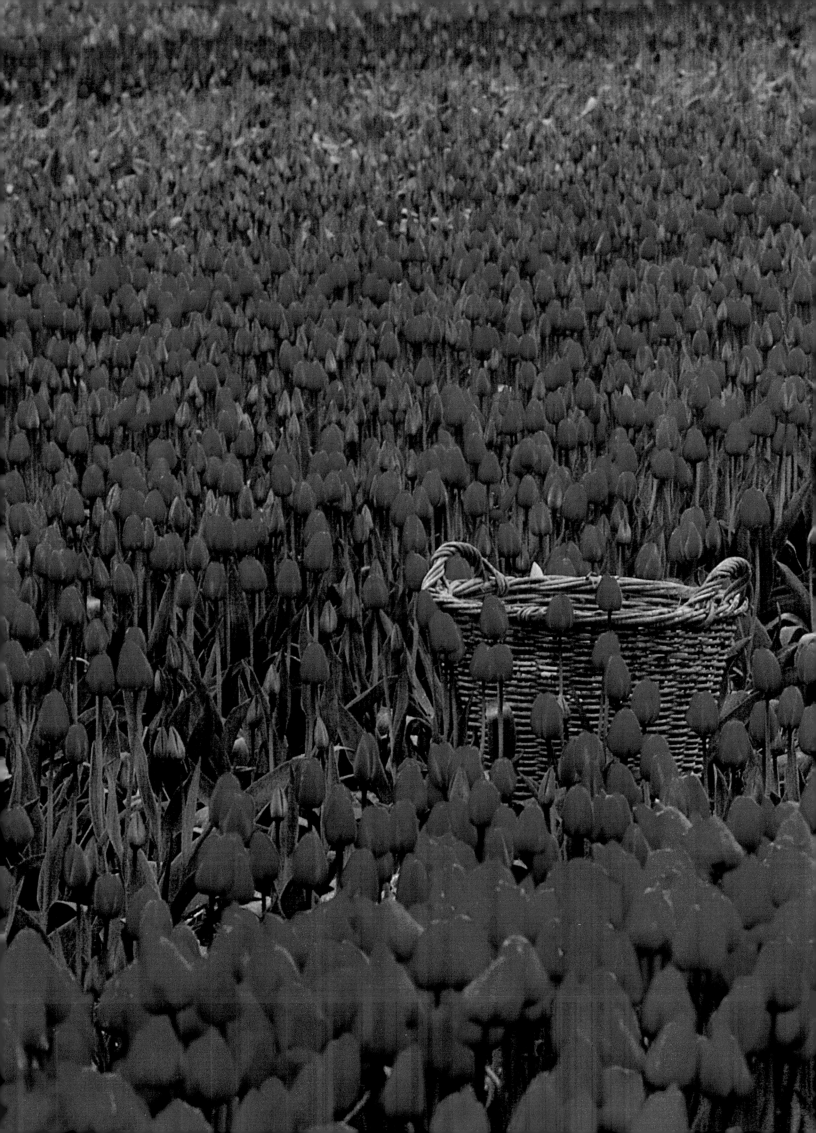

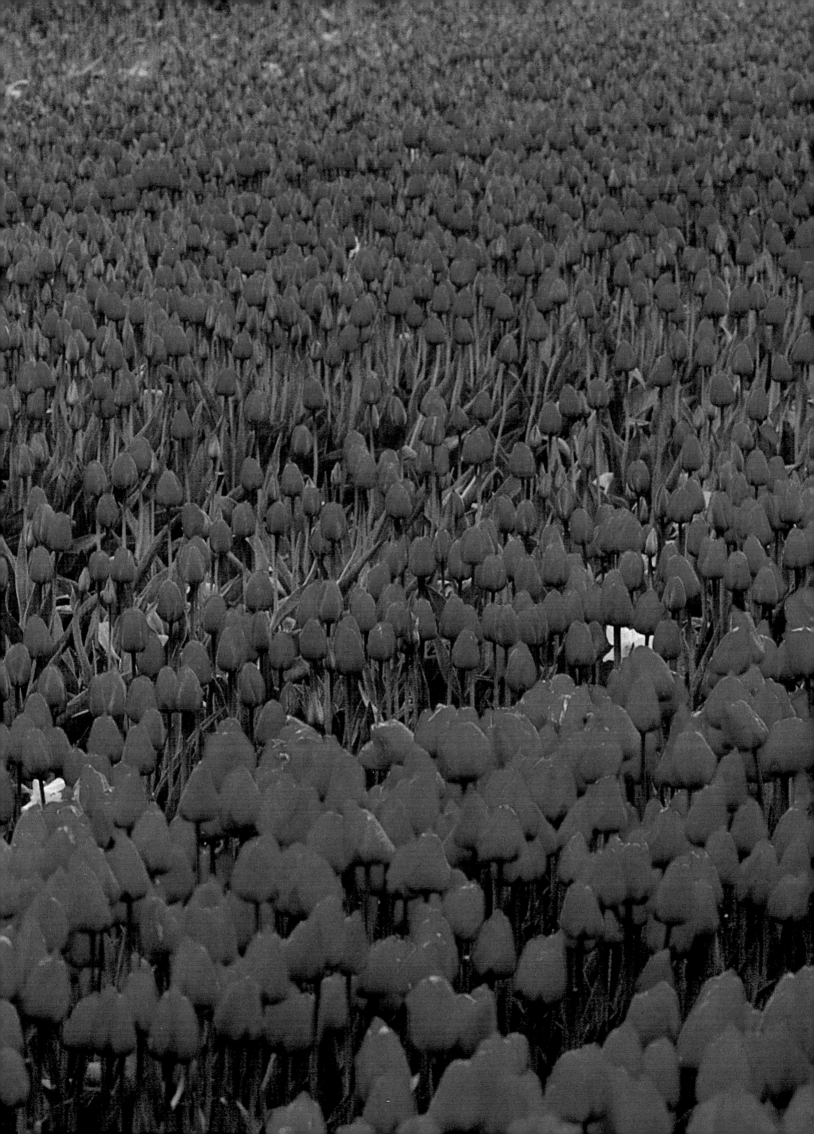

The Gypsy and the Garden

Italian gardens are hidden worlds: guarded, ringed with massive walls, closed. How often I heard the word *chiuso* from the gatekeeper while tantalizing glimpses of balustrades and bright geraniums, moss-softened statuary, and umbrella pines beckoned from behind the locked iron gates.

I tried to assuage my discouragement with a good meal in the old city of Lucca. As I left the restaurant a woman wearing a boldly colored scarf and a backpack asked for money for herself and her children. She was not old but her eyes were hard and weary. I gave her what small change I had.

"Grazie, signore" — she would tell me my fortune. Tracing the lines on my palm with a jagged fingernail, she revealed the full mystery of my life's story in a language I did not understand. Just as well.

She continued to hold on to my hand and her eyes grew harder still. For a ridiculous sum she would promise me success in *amore* and all other endeavors, if I refused she would give me the curse of the evil eye — *"il malocchio."* It was a beautiful afternoon; the food had been good and the wine was taking effect, of course I would pay her. She pulled a hair from my head, blew on it, and placed it in my palm. Another burst of unintelligible Italian followed — a benediction or a curse? We parted.

The following morning I approached a villa's garden with the usual trepidation, climbing up the dusty road to the ochre-colored farmhouse that stood before the gates. The last roses of the season bloomed in the doorway, and birds in wooden cages — finches and canaries pouring forth song — were hung outside an open window like wash to catch the morning sun. An old woman sat in a chair by the wall, knitting.

"Chiuso," she said, "It is closed." My disappointment was evident. She studied me awhile and then, covering her eyes with one hand, she gestured toward the gate, as if to say "Go ahead in. I never saw you." The gypsy's charm was working. I went in.

Playing God

Imagine, if you can, having an army of two hundred men, shovels in hand, digging serpentine lakes, changing the course of streams, and moving whole hills. Imagine covering the entire floor of an oak forest with bluebells, or, if flamboyant colors are more to your taste, a lavish underplanting of flamelike azaleas. Imagine searching the world for the choicest rhododendrons from the Himalayas, the most delicate-leaved Japanese maples, the progeny of the tallest North American sequoias, and placing them wherever you wanted, so that they might grow for no other purpose than to please your eye.

Imagine being able to do with the land whatever you wished, reforming it, remolding it, and replanting it to your own vision — playing God. And imagine, to continue this wishful thinking, bringing into your creation flocks of white doves, iridescent Indian peafowl filling the woods with their exotic cries, and shy herds of fallow deer moving fleetingly through the landscape with the sound and motion of swiftly flowing water.

Imagine yourself a landed aristocrat or a powerful baron of industry in Victorian England, and you might have done all these things. In the eighteenth and nineteenth centuries, England had the immense wealth — concentrated in a few self-indulgent and restless hands — and the burning desire to create wooded and open landscape gardens with little compromise. Of course, playing God without the benefit of divine omniscience has its pitfalls. But where the conception was clear and the hand stopped short of excess, as at Petworth, or Wakehurst, or Stourhead, gardens of God-like beauty were born.

Imagine the risks of attempting to enhance and control the natural landscape on this scale. Only men with the confidence engendered by such infinite wealth would be audacious enough to try, and only men who, while playing God, still practiced some human restraint and humility, would be sensible enough to succeed.

Epilogue

Photography for me has always been an act of affirmation. Each time the shutter is released it is a way of saying, Yes, this is something I am intrigued by, moved by, something worth keeping and worth validating, if only in this limited way. When I photograph a garden, I am simply trying to point out what I respond to most strongly.

While looking through a camera lens is not quite the same as seeing a garden naturally, through unfettered eyes, it forces me to take the time to become more intensely aware of the visual patterns, the interplay of light and colors, and the small clues to the garden's larger meaning that might lie hidden there. The more time I spend photographing gardens, the more I am captivated by these clues and their cultural contexts. Why are the evergreens in Japanese gardens so painstakingly pruned to resemble idealized versions of themselves, and why in English gardens are they often pruned to resemble just the opposite: pyramids or globes, or even roosters? Why do French gardens favor the rose and Holland's the tulip. Why, at Versailles, is the goal to have a limitless view, and at Tenjuan to see infinity in the immediate rocks and plants and sand? The answer, of course, is that cultures are a collective people's voice, and each of these cultural voices has its own inflection. The fascination lies in trying to figure out if, ultimately, all the different voices are saying the same thing: that expressed in all gardens is the universal longing for paradise, for a more perfect harmony between man and the natural world.

In a way, I, too, have felt like a gardener — perhaps most like those nineteenth-century English gardener-collectors who scoured the world for exotic plants — as I have searched in various cultures for those garden elements that were to me most essential and intriguing, and they have taken root in my own vision of what Eden might be.

List of Photographs

Technical Information

The photographs in this book were taken with Nikon F2 cameras and the following lenses: 28mm, 55mm, 105mm, and 200mm. For this kind of work I use a tripod whenever possible, and, for maximum depth of field, exposures were often one second or more. The film used was Kodachrome 25 or 64.